WHO LET THE CAT OUT OF THE BAG?

Written and illustrated by fourth-grade students of
Newcastle Avenue Elementary in Reseda, California

SCHOLASTIC INC.
New York Toronto London Auckland Sydney Mexico City New Delhi Hong Kong

Copyright © 2002 by Scholastic Inc
Scholastic and associated logos are trademarks and/or registered trademarks of Scholastic Inc
ISBN 0-439-44619-8

12 11 10 9 8 7 6 5 4 3 2 1   00 01 02 03 04

Book Design by Bill Henderson
Printed and bound in the U.S.A.

First Printing, July 2002

Meet the Authors

First Row: Haik Abdunuryan, Cindy Almendarez, Ariana Ascencio, Francisco Avitia, Norbert Buza, Carlos Castillo, Carlos Castro, Cody Cocolotta, Adan Colmenares

Second Row: Stephanie Fuentes, Ruby Gonzlez, Angel Jimenez, Nicole Jovel, Greta Lara, Jessica Linares, Luiz Luna, Jesus Magana, Diana Martinez

Third Row: Ms. Lizette Madruga, Eduardo Mena, Natalie Moran, Catherine Perez, Mirna Serratos, Dillon Smith, Megan Smith, David Soriano, Matthew Taghavi, Diego Valdez, Ms. Carlyn Taggart

Don't put your foot in your mouth.

Meaning: Be careful what you say.

I have ants in my pants.

Meaning: I'm so excited that I can't sit still.

You're driving me up the wall.

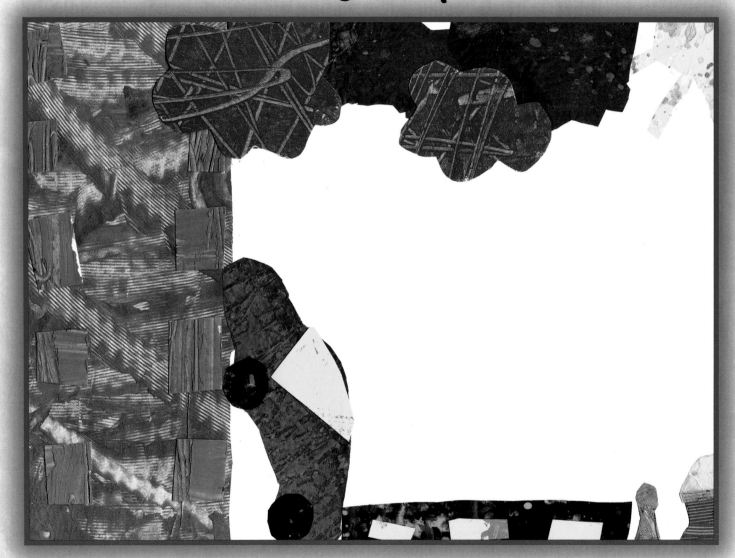

Meaning: You're making me crazy.

Who let the cat out of the bag?

Meaning: Who told the secret?

You're barking up the wrong tree.

Meaning: Whatever you're looking for, you won't find it here.

Don't spill the beans.

Meaning: Don't tell the secret.

Cut it out.

Meaning: Stop what you are doing and behave.

Time flies.

Meaning: Time goes by quickly.

He woke up on the wrong side of the bed.

Meaning: He woke up grouchy and grumpy.

I'm all ears.

Meaning: I am paying attention to you.

Don't count your chickens before they hatch.

Meaning: Don't expect something to happen until it really happens.

The cat got your tongue.

Meaning: You forgot what you were going to say.

Food's on me.

Meaning: I will pay for our meals.

They have hearts of gold.

Meaning: They are courteous, considerate, and thoughtful.

They're couch potatoes.

Meaning: They watch a lot of TV and are lazy.

She thinks money grows on trees.

Meaning: She spends a lot of money.

She took the words right out of my mouth.

Meaning: She said what I was going to say.

Lend me a hand.

Diego Valdez

Meaning: Can you help me?

She has a green thumb.

Meaning: She is a good gardener. Her plants live long and grow tall.

Don't rain on my parade.

Meaning: Don't ruin my happy moments.

Don't cry over spilt milk.

Eduardo Mena

Meaning: Don't worry about what happened in the past, because you can't change it.

You paid an arm and a leg.

Meaning: You spent a lot of money.

You're pulling my leg.

Meaning: You're playing a joke on me.

You're in the hot seat.

Meaning: You're in trouble.

Zip your lips.

Meaning: Be quiet and close your mouth.

Let's hit the road.

Meaning: Let's get moving; let's go.

It's raining cats and dogs.

Meaning: It's raining very hard.

"The future belongs
to those who believe
in the beauty
of their dreams."

Eleanor Roosevelt

Kids Are Authors ®
Books written by children for children

The Kids Are Authors ® Competition was established in 1986 to encourage children to read and to become involved in the creative process of writing. Since then, thousands of children have written and illustrated books as participants in the Kids Are Authors ® Competition. The winning books in the annual competition are published by Scholastic Inc. and are distributed by Scholastic Book Fairs throughout the United States.

For more information:
Kids Are Authors ®
P O Box 958411
Lake Mary, FL 32795-8411

Or visit our web site at:
www.scholasticbookfairs.com